RACKETS & BATTERIES
CHRISTOPHER GUTKIND

NEWTON-LE-WILLOWS

Published in the United Kingdom in 2026
by The Knives Forks And Spoons Press,
51 Pipit Avenue,
Newton-le-Willows,
Merseyside,
WA12 9RG.

ISBN 978-1-916590-15-1

Copyright © Christopher Gutkind 2026.

The right of Christopher Gutkind to be identified as the author of this work has been asserted by them in accordance with the Copyrights, Designs and Patents Act of 1988. All rights reserved. No part of this publication may be reproduced, stored in a retrieval system, transmitted in any form or by any means, electronic, photocopying, recording or otherwise, without prior permission of the publisher.

Acknowledgements:

I am grateful to the editors of the following publications for publishing some of these poems: *Shadowtrain, Shearsman, Eonta, Ravaged Wonderful Earth: A Collection for David Kessel, The Stumbling Dance, In Between Hangovers, Poetry Salzburg Review, Barking Dogs, Kater Murr's Piraeus Series, Red Ceilings, Camellia, Fire, Straight From The Fridge, Shrug Magazine, Great Works, The Bizarre Tambourine, The [SOAS] Spirit, Poetry is Dead, Morning Star, Desperate Literature, DATABLEED, Pamenar, Mercurius, Corroding the Now, Kruk Book, Writers Forum e-zine.*

Many thanks to Alec Newman and Knives Forks Spoons for publishing this, family and friends and poets I know, mostly in London, and to the poetry organizers.

Other books: *Inside to Outside*, Shearsman 2006
Options, with artist Trevor Simmons, Knives Forks Spoons 2010
Digits After Orph, Veer Books 2025

Cover photo, *A Pox Upon You*, by Jeff Hilson. Ta Jeff!

cgutkind@yahoo.com

Rackets & Batteries

Tale
American Street
Still
Wintering
Remember Today
25 Years Later
Options in Third to Last Line of *Middle of Computer*
COMings
London
Desert Island Bliss
Not Iraq (2003)
Greetings
As I Left …
'At the End of the Day'
Park
Gliding with the Hitler Youth
Time
Stroke
Ahoy!
Thinking
Sisyphus
Making the World Better
£10 / 10 Years Old
Fuckers
Here and There
In Sausalito
Plea
Dark Song
Grey to Stay
Crick Institute
Computered
Poem-to-Machine
Comfuse
Everyday to Hide
Late
Wind
Badanjiling
Opened
40 (SF to LA)
Shifting Over Her
Battery
Racket
dc memorial
Seeds
[nothing]

Notes

***Snot save our hideous sheen,
long shits our ruling mean.***

(ON A LONDON WALL)

Tale

this is the outernet
or maybe it's the internet
just another internet
and you out in the outernet
tending to the internet
while I go off in outernet
just another outernet
speaking out an internet
or ...

American Street

man walking down the street
keep on walking
thank you

car turning left over there
keep turning left
and then disappear please yes very good

squirrel sitting on that branch
eating a nut
keep eating that nut

air letting me walk into you
keep letting me in
keep letting me
cheers

you group of friends talking and laughing
one of you suddenly go off
yes exactly like that
good

policemen watching and protecting some
sure maybe follow that guy

person playing with their dog
throwing a ball
and shouting
keep playing that way
that's right

lights changing from green to red
don't stop changing
first yellow and now red
perfect

cars gradually slowing down
keep doing that
and then stop thank you

old woman voting in the school
keep voting
yes you're right the election isn't fair
that's just the way it goes

blue sky with a few clouds
stay blue like that
but go dark later when you should
don't forget

house over there with nice windows
keep standing and don't fall
you'll be fine

plane in the sky keep flying

woman walking
but then stopping to think
of your mother
keep thinking about her
excellent

tiny fly landing on me
stay there
and now no now
fly away

lemons on the tree I'm passing
turn yellow
and then drop some day

tree-tops swaying and brushed by the wind
keep swaying like that
and wind you keep brushing them
thank you

and you two
falling in love over there
with your eyes and voices stroking each other
keep going in please
keep going

man with a gun in your car
think about using it
or imagine being shot
your choice

girl coming out of supermarket
yes go to your car
open door
perfect

engine let yourself be started
don't resist
just go with it

cat on those stairs all curled up
stayed curled up
that's right

music vibrating by now
slow down and push
into our heads
and out our asses
nice one

and buildings off to the side
spot me close by
and then look closer
that's better

and people behind glass
behind computers
working in there
people making better bombs
to keep us safe
keep making them
without fear
fantastic

and almost empty bar
I'm passing
later fill up with joy please

mailman putting mail through
all those nice doors
keep doing that
always do that
thank you

boy walking towards me
yes stop and tie your shoe very good
and now keep coming
towards me

leaf hanging there
oh okay
fall off now
and float to the ground
no problem

rich man across the street scared of everything
stay scared like that
no you can't pay for it to stop

another girl leaving supermarket
not going to a car
yes just walk home

guy over there turning left no right
sure go that way instead

dogs I told you to play
not fight
stop please

ball bouncing down the street
keep doing that
good good good

green lawns scattered
here and there
don't worry
you'll be together again someday

missiles going over there
what are you doing
coming back?

man wandering in a circle by those trees
keep wandering

ball suddenly back up here
yes okay
you can come back and play

politician talking on tv
with the expert
and the host
all lie and seem reasonable please
and more tomorrow
perfect

fake flamingos dressed-up like astronauts
stay like that awhile
don't suddenly change
you're not allowed to

nice flowers blooming and happy
keep blooming like that
but then stop in a few days
when you feel like it
or if you get tired

lady begging on the corner
keep begging I guess
yes things will mostly be like this
no there's nothing
I can do

firemen rushing to a fire
keep rushing

family in that house eating
keep eating
and something exploding you all to pieces now
keep exploding
that's right
that was supposed to happen
too

but people screaming and racing towards me
stop screaming
stop racing
now stop!

ah very good
man walking with a kind of skip
keep doing that

but you
you stop that over there
no need to hit him
why don't you stop?

friend walking beside me
keep walking beside me
you will keep walking beside me
won't you?

and bird falling out of the sky
stop falling now

and apple please taste like an apple again

and words doing less
go away
stop stopping me

but me walking up the street
keep walking

but me walking up the street
keep dreaming

but me walking up the street
keep

Still

If you should be inside
the British Museum
go to the Parthenon Galleries holding
the sculptures
we stole.

If you have time walk by them very slowly
and take care to look
especially at the faces that have
crumbled away.

I went there to try ...

Zeus is gone but much of Poseidon's
great torso remains
and still seems to move with all the containment
of an ocean.

Go look and walk slowly there
before we disappear
or get ourselves uploaded
and haven't eyes
to touch them.

Wintering

The offerings of the conversations
around us, the wind in lives of friends
who skate off inside you, the winter
traffic easing further into its convulsion
of beginning speech, this might be a
night I have if I need it, this might make
my next waking day a birthday of the
possible, the whispers and oil of daylight
dreams, everything still hanging from
the words we make to settle, weather us,
explore from in contagions of delight
or despair, face between want and reply,
you drifty in the air that breathes me
in slow race with yourself I never see.

Remember Today

Your moments of silence
cannot be heard.
Your red poppies drip.
Your efforts are stillborn.
Your memories fail
to lead you elsewhere.

So you keep it to once a year.

25 Years Later

a giant fake poppy
flattened and stickered
on front of trains

it's not a poppy

someone devised this
migration from our chests

a poppy is more

some kinds of killing
have approval made for them,
their designers too

and very ancient

it stands like a target
growing stronger

it lives without us

observance grows wider,
allows mourning
to make new bullets

a poppy is better

the future is the same
as the past la-la

and grows-up

in its red and black
we replant war

you're in it

OPTIONS IN THIRD TO LAST LINE OF MIDDLE OF COMPUTER

open the app to twitsigh
twit our appeyes to sigh
twittle appeyes and sigh
twit open doors and sigh
twit open the app to sigh
shut the twits and sigh
twittle to speak appsigh
go twittling sighs to appeye
go all twittly for appsigh
go twittling our appeyes
twittle doors for appsigh
shut twittles and appsigh
shut twittle for appeyes
open twittle for appeyes
open twittle and appsigh
shut the apps by twitsigh
open the app by twithigh
shut open the twit to sigh
twittle our long appsigh
twittle our long appeyes
twittle our short appeyes
twittlefeed the twiteyes
feed twittly the appeyes
sigh twittly appyfeedyeyes
twittle the doors to sigh

COMINGS

I.com love you
I love.com you
I love you.com

I.com hate you
I hate.com you
I hate you.com

I.com buy you
I buy.com you
I buy you.com

I.com sell you
I sell.com you
I sell you.com

etc
you do more
please

London

I loved being in your rooms
and on your streets
under your roof of cloud

and when the grey gave way
all your shifting histories
circled up into the deep light blue,

that wondering blue
almost every heart
would be glad to be made of.

. . .

I looked into your centres
and took journeys
in your busloads of languages,

got caught in your wishing-well
of faces and sat still
in damp flats by pale gasfires,

hearing everything everywhere
hiss together so-so
while passing through.

. . .

And on some dull winter day
I'd stroll the parks,
picking out shapes of us

through the dark leafless trees,
reeling in your wide
silences and far enough

from our new machines,
always calling
us back for feeding.

Desert Island Bliss

No one mentioned the island was ours,
   that we lived so alone
from each other in ourselves.

No one came back asking if
   we're better now, if we dive in and out
and listen - listening too

is solitary - on our gull-guided vessel,
   anchored to be eased,
dreaming creatures bound

to feel at home, hardly saying
   what we need aboard.
Then the image drowns, stays too sunk

to see - fantasy a desert
   above one's own - it's better alone
away from home.

Not Iraq (2003)

Destruction is fun.
A few of us stopped today
to watch it happening,
the walls splintering and collapsing,
glass flying, waves of dust,
the past thinning out.

The cinema was being torn down,
they'd build a new one,
and the memories inside,
the awe, the mixed revelations,
all those silent stares?
Who knows, who cares.

I looked around at the empty air
and suddenly felt larger,
but weak, more alone.
Later a pile of mangled rubble
was all that remained –
there was no one in there.

GREETINGS

A young girl
puts her name on the missile
to say hello,
this is from me ...

Soldiers usually do this ...

Her handwriting is very beautiful,
she holds the pen
very carefully,
like a knife ...

Other words say
With Love ...

Mother looks on,
she's relieved,
happy to have turned fear
into delight ...

This is magic being prepared ...

What fun this is,
let's take a picture,
let's remember this moment
for years to come ...

There they go,
the smiles ...

As the missile flies
in no one's sky
does the air
feel her touch?

There they go, here they come ...

As the missile
slices someone open
do they read
her lovely name?

Do they feel the fun
going in?

My hello is your goodbye,
my smile is your cry,
I've got a better
name than you ...

As I Left ...

As I left the ATM
with a friend.
As I left the ATM
I looked back—I don't know why.
As I left the ATM
it happened—I regret it.
As I left the ATM
it was the worst thing.
As I left the ATM
everything fell and crashed for us.
As I left the ATM
I'll tell you—I will I will.
As I left the ATM
our life was over then.
As I left the ATM
damn me it happened
damn me for looking back.
As I left the ATM
where was God then?
where were my senses?
As I left the ATM
I didn't think—didn't think I'm telling you!
As I left the ATM
it just happened—just came out.
As I left the ATM
why this—why this of all things?
As I left the ATM
what are we to do now?
As I left the ATM
we were just walking away.
As I left the ATM
why didn't I just keep walking?
As I left the ATM
I turned—somehow I turned.
As I left the ATM
the worst thing in the world.
As I left the ATM
I'm going to tell you I will
I'm building it.

As I left the ATM
I need to shock you
—will you be?
As I left the ATM
please be please be upset.
As I left the ATM
I turned and get ready now.
As I left the ATM
I turned to that fucking machine.
As I left the ATM
I turned and said—*thank you.*

As I left the ATM
it's true—it is it really is.
As I left the ATM
what's happening?
what's happening to us?
As I left the ATM
fuck me for this fuck me.
As I left the ATM
I turned and I spoke to it I did.
As I left the ATM
I said it and then heard it
—but so what?
As I left the ATM
I heard it and stopped
and all the world broke.
As I left the ATM
I wanted to cry
but I laughed—so what?
As I left the ATM
you know what happened now.
As I left the ATM
March 24 2005
with a friend.

'AT THE END OF THE DAY'

At the end of the day I'm still here, still here,
but I'm not sure that I want to be, or why.
Our world's about to end, everything we hold dear.

The mind spins its wheels, stuck in what it hears,
and personal things, like phones, make me cry.
At the end of the day I'm still here, still here,

out the door and off to work year after year,
scaling my own height, falling back on the lies.
Our world's about to end, everything we hold dear.

Our leaders and schemers deny the end is near,
nukes will never be used, the sea won't rise to the sky.
At the end of the day I'm still here, still here,

there's no need for us to stop or change gears,
there's only the need to believe you can fly.
Our world's about to end, everything we hold dear.

And many, perhaps most, will drift in tears.
No longer will we shut the door and sigh
at the end of the day: *I'm still here, still here.*
Our world's about to end, everything we hold dear.

Park

    before fall trees being full
        leaves tend green
      song swings true

    before fall one day going
        friends kiss about
      skies lean blue

    during fall wind not alone
        colour tears away
      debris gets born

    after fall passing escapes
        easy sighted kites
      kept lost in place

    after fall seeing through
        branchy whisks
      hold *if* proof

G<small>LIDING WITH THE</small> H<small>ITLER</small> Y<small>OUTH</small>

But look at the delicate way
    they hold their craft,
  the way they want their constructions
    to float now,

to fly away from them,
    a responsibility getting lighter, leaving.
And the way they're all in a line,
    the kids, their planes

and behind them, organizing officials,
    even the parents perhaps,
  watching too, waiting for that apprehensive moment
    their child,

so suddenly poised,
    tightens back and pushes away,
the thin, boney thing leaving their hands,
    pointing as it goes

to what they seem to be gazing at,
    its trail, its target,
to what they're able to see for certain,
    only that,

not what they can't see,
    what they can't believe now,
  other places, other kids,
    other planes.

TIME

Never think the one
who has gone
isn't there

yesterday is always going on
always happening
like it did

you two are still walking
next to each other
before this

never think it's only in you
because that was then
and this is now

because whatever happens tomorrow
you'll still be in today

it's just over there
just over your
shoulder

it's the only bridge
we can't go
back on

you can't
touch it

but it's
there.

STROKE

I was worded, I had no food.
   It continues a theme
but I can't contribute.
   My tongue's dry, it doesn't speak.
I'm losing myself again,
   another makes me.

My image is broken,
   it can't see now.
I need no mirror, its cracks
   scrape inside, itching
spreads this ink
   in patterns I find
   beautiful.

Let's go, to silence.
   Its sifting outlines pull us to fill
another time. It fits well.
   This isn't magic in a dream.
I reach a porous spread
   of courses believed, invented, given.

Hands replace my face
   but only when
I don't look close, don't open
   it up. Otherwise,
ordinary moments will
   stare teeming
   but helpless.

On the menu of nothing
   I try. A mouth still opens,
attention waits, picks
   a suggestion. It can't be helped
with food about, a myth
   I am partially.

An expert cut ends rough.
   My image is cast
by others. Small figures
   walk into place
in a cry and sense.
   If I alter too much
   I'll see me.

Ahoy!

I.com love you
I really do.com
it's.com a lot to ask
but will you be
my.com you.com
one day too?

remember when
we fell in.com love
but now maybe
we really love.com
each.com other

our parents.com
should know it
and maybe when
we we.com too
they'll know.com it
deep4.0 inside

I heard it works
like that.com

it's nice.com
if.com it's true.com
and not just
some old tale

see.com later
kiss.com
upon your neck
like you
like.com

sleep soft
if you rest.com
after all this
semi com
will be.com better
next time
more com

can't wait
for youcom!

etc

Thinking

They should build more trees
   I thought driving,
after I finally saw some on this highway
   of few trees.

And I thought
   they should make more cows here
after I saw only a few
   of them too.

And clouds,
   they need to put some puffy ones in
and let them wander,
   not too many.

And a lake,
   they should load a nice one
for people to swim in
   if they want.

Then maybe they will do
   these things
I thought.

Sisyphus

you don't push a rock
without success
so it rushes past you again

but twice a day everyday
you push and pull
three trolleys in turn

up the street in the afternoon
and back late at night
to and from somewhere you come and go

slowly using all your strength
though you continue
to have more to use up

and past us and our views
you remain there
to remind us of losing

so we can't shelve you
and walk away
to be unfollowed

but I do

Making the World Better

There was tremendous sadness and suffering and anxiety everywhere and maybe only a small number of people were happy and without worry.

Then up in the sky smoke started to form and get thicker and be pulled into a small part of the world where the air smelled bad and dusty and where it was always busy and crazy like too many thoughts.

You could see workers emptying huge trucks of broken and pulverized concrete and glass and filling up big wheelbarrows and buckets and shovels and then spreading this and large pieces of bent metal over the ground and in several giant holes.

And some people living near there had always been filled with an expanding death-grief for someone they knew and maybe loved without ever meeting but after a few more days they felt a little hopeful so they wandered around looking and asking after them by holding their picture and crying until they completely broke down with fear and worry.

And over several days and nights even more smoke and dust came from the sky and spread everywhere but most went to that area where the air was thick and sticky and grey and where it was getting difficult to breathe.

And sometimes a person who was all dead or maybe just a small piece that was left of them would be brought to the broken area and put tenderly in one of the holes and then covered up with rubble.

And in nearby homes or places of work everyone was mostly agitated or subdued but some went to hospitals to be filled with a little blood and then they stood around as if they had to wait awhile before walking properly again.

Meanwhile the broken stuff kept coming until the holes finally grew small and disappeared and then became mountains of smashed-up chairs and desks and doors and computers and also chunks of bodies and phones and carpets and ceilings and all of it carefully mixed together as though it mattered.

It even happened a few times that some very injured person was put into what seemed a special place which the workers then covered and watched over with great concern before shouting into that spot some sort of desperate farewell.

Then over the next day it got more frantic in that part of town until suddenly it looked as though everyone was rushing to be there like they didn't want to miss something and some of them chased a dirty giant cloud of warm smoke which was the size of many buildings.

And many people seemed to want to go where those first dead or hurt people went and where it was now all smoke and crashing and fire-smell and mixed-up with sirens and screams and almost everyone who went deep in there started shouting and screaming and crying too.

Some were even limping or bleeding but if they asked others to help them lie down and let them be then it appeared they were getting better painfully with their scrapes and bumps and burns lessening and even disappearing.

*What is this place
that had such power?*

But then fast like a real surprise all that dust and debris and noise rolled up and combined with bone-bits and muscle and the memories of those soon to be to make an incredibly tall and already-peopled building with shafts of fire coming out of it while dark smoke blew from its top like a warning.

*Is this what everyone
was rushing to do?*

And often some sad soul who was dead and bloody and bent strange over the ground would somehow start themselves and shoot up very far and perfect into a broken window where maybe they'd wave and wander off into a smoky or even fiery bit and sometimes the window would repair itself behind them.

On the streets below it was chaos and most people were dazed by what was happening but others who could still think okay rushed towards the police and firefighters who helped them through all the smoke and some still rising debris into the almost finished building.

For a short time the air felt a bit lighter but then there were more screams and crashings and dense grey smoke and choking dust with crowds rushing into it until it also rolled up and grew into a second tall building exactly like the other one except for its particular people and it gleamed slightly like it was celebrating its creation out of these great and painful and impossible efforts.

And all the while as this second tower rose a panicky hush overcame everyone watching as though it might not quite uncrush and complete itself but in the end it did and just like the first one it was finished off with deep flashings of fire and plumes of lovely black smoke.

And on the ground it got busier than ever and as chunks of metal and glass flew up to find their places they often took people's cuts and bruises away while they rushed and escaped into the buildings like they were late for work or a long-awaited show of some sort.

And everyone who went inside instantly became especially scared and upset as if being out in all the madness was better for them but they just went in anyway.

And in each building many floors were filled with smoke or fire and it was a fire so hot that whole offices and halls and toilets and even human beings somehow bubbled into existence out of nothing with the people sometimes choking themselves awake or leaping out of the fire and screaming as if horror at their own birthing before others gathered around who perhaps were also newly made and who could welcome and reassure them which they sometimes did by screaming and other times by crying softly nearby.

And it seemed like there were thousands of people scrambling to be part of this with everyone wanting to get in there even though it terrified them but some were so desperate they'd run up twenty or forty or sixty floors to get where they felt they belonged.

But then it became clear some other fantastic work was being done in there and that those towers were a kind of hidden factory with each producing after several spectacular explosions a complete airplane with new but already living people inside them and each plane was shot out fast and high by a last fire they instantly extinguished though they were still welcomed with endless screams that quickly died away both inside and outside the towers and maybe even inside the planes which like magic put in place the last missing windows as they left and flew off soon after each other into a beautiful blue day.

And a great and almost unnoticed ease was suddenly felt through the city but especially among those who earlier had so desperately sought their lost friends and loved ones but now didn't worry as much.

And all that seemed to remain of this series of incredible events was the still to be fully understood cause of what happened and the shocked state of those fortunate ones inside those amazing planes but even they grew more relaxed approaching their first destination.

Maybe things really can get better.

£10.00 / 10 Years Old

He gave his all
to help a poor people.
The poor people
accepted his all and it helped.

He heard the news
and felt a need to change things.
Changing things
was far beyond
what he could do.

In his innocence
he didn't demand a fairer world
but merely gave his all.
A fair world
would find his innocence
enough.

Fuckers

    They're a bunch of covidlers
          meanwhile
    They're covidling the accounts
          all the dead
    They're telling huge covidlies
          and injured

    They covidled our fake news
          meanwhile
    They don't give a slaver's covidle
          all the used
    They play covidles for laughs
          more used

Here and There

Behind the building next to mine
there is a woman living outside

who everyday tries to feed a little cat,
approaches it with a slightly anxious

but tender seriousness, her hand holding out
a tin of food, the cat always hesitant,

not letting her get too close, so she has to
leave it there and quietly back away ...

And she seems to so want to care for it,
care for some little living piece of life,

feel closer and closer to it, that she almost
can't bear to put down her offerings

without some sort of acknowledgement
that she too exists, that she too needs

some bit of life to look at her, reach out
just for her before going away again ...

Yet eventually she lays down the morsels
and steps aside, and eventually the cat

goes to them, eats and disappears again,
and then I disappear as well, outside,

and then she disappears too, off to collect
bottles and cans and cash them in –

but eventually she returns, puts down
her bedding, waits for the next day,

waits for everything the world has
to offer, everything it can't be,

everything it should be, again
and again all over the place.

In Sausalito

There's the feeling this is where a pent-up
horrific massacre might happen.

There's a tall twisting wall of homes
surrounding the bay below –
most are on stilts so ground floors are the top of houses.
Sometimes a Ferrari parks on one.

Often the hills are too steep for a garden
so the children play inside.
Sometimes there's a little Buddha sitting out front
like someone's calling-card.

Down in the town daytrippers get off ferries
and go over to Starbucks
to wake-up and feel at home.

Galleries of 'arts and crafts' decorate the place.
Glass dolphins and Klimt
rip-offs look out behind alarms.

Locals shop at a changing backstreet where
tourists are quickly sniffed out.

And there's a houseboat in the marina modelled
on the Taj Mahal that people look at.

It all looks like someone didn't think well.
As though someone might
come in and shoot up the town.

Plea

In the chess and chance I'm calling,
not exactly but still slightly still,
asking and even believing I can reach you

without too much of an introduction.
I might give a sentence of myself,
my altered life yawning and you could look

your way, in your time, not exactly
but still just enough to stand by.
Porously I sound, in hope, ready to be hooked

and yet almost desiring to bait you:
off and on I float without serving.
Maybe one day I'll board you without a cut
only if you call me by guessing.

Dark Song

Dark pain inside me.
Hole in my heart.
Where were you before?
I never noticed you,
I never felt you before.

Dear hole inside me,
do you have a name?
I knew but didn't know.
I don't want to hurt her anymore,
I've hurt her too much.

Deep hole, so dark,
I can't see what's in there.
Nothing. Pure endless nothing.
You're indestructible.
As hope, as hopelessness.

You're all that's left of her,
you and the memory,
my love that fools me,
lessens you but makes you grow.
That is how I breathe.

Dark hole inside me.
What do you say?
Nothing. Only time.
A language I never knew.
My own language.

GREY TO STAY

Look –
   up in the sky
     is a plain-
   ness you
      can hardly
         say by.

Trying
   it I'll try
    too
   bring
    the grey
   into view –

grey
   about life
     speckling
   with a few
    zebras
      to cross by.

If we
   or at least
    I
     do find relief
 or get
    scared

with these
    things
    continually
       treading –
it's enough
   to get across

for now
    what we are
without
   wasting
what we're
   less of.

    . . .

As a
   bee sees
      so x whys
z – both
      count down
     the road –

to speak
     or ask
   dreaming
       though
        the buzz
    is riskier

more stung
     you see –
   that's all
    a sky
   so far
so clear so

near
  and proud away
      from asking
       itself
    the answer
    kept.

And why do I
   tend to
    ignore
      so many zebras
   crossing
    easily

to join
  less and less –
      does fear
    take me past
      their dicey
        look?

Chances there
    and choices
      from
    the leaning.
There –
  see how

they smile
   the four-limbed
     cre-
    ative ones
   who've
arrived

to meet me
     soon as
  I depart
from grey
  asides
    exactly.

     . . .

Now that
  is hard-
    ly the way
to make me
    grow
   hooves

I felt
  like saying
but
  stopped
     myself so
   succeeding.

It's well
    this simple joust
  is tiring
    enough
to concede
    inability

if the sky
  won't
    be met
   as it brings
   me
     to try –

so I ride
   another
   zebra
     settling
    with
its crowd

watching
  but
   not
  feeling
 my weight
  yet.

Crick Institute

They're making us there,
like somebody goes in,
something else comes out
with the same name.

The possibilities are endless.

They'll crick us in there,
fore-face to ass-after,
mining and/or, dancing dna in/over,
cell-money bits 'n measures,
new chains nullifying,
bio-tool transition recipes
building off our was.

The possibilities to end us.

Who is in and who is out,
a spawning of classes,
othering everything but self
yet tightly automatic
and far-intimate again,
the ark of everything
to buy and sell you,
fleshing in and outward
before fleshing off.

COMPUTERED

I go into the computer,
seem to leave myself outside.

Inside me the system plays soft .coms
or deals they want me
and maybe just me to feel.

Around me are other people,
vaguely or really there, shopping.
Around me other products we bot home.

I step into the aisle of lives they call data.
I look wavery, feeling dizzy, uneasy.
So many: a thousand, maybe five thousand varieties.

I can't find the one I want.
Too bad they don't have more,
one more, mine.

I walk out. I seem to rejoin myself.
People wander, apps go by,
in the greater market called community.

They have made it look real
so it's supposed to be like this.

POEM-TO-MACHINE

Take some poetry,
574352186724.
Take something you feel
in wires or whatnot,
take a shot – I'm giving you it!
20149528279516.
Feel better now?
Going great now?
Here's some love for you,
872241056398!
Here's a vacation,
0000000000!
Here's your next job,
44016229!

Comfuse

The computer went in the life
but it did not come out.
    Then another computer went in the next life
but it did not come out either.

    It's like computer and life were made
for each other, had spent all
    their energy for this and could
die now, feeling completed.

    While in streetscom over the world
most of us just kept watching,
    half-expecting the computers to app out again,
but they didn't, they just detailed in.

    Then the lives retailed away,
tendered into the databurbs
    as dreamybots, taking what they knew
with them, their labour and loves,

    their yesterday, today, tomorrow,
friends, family, loads, codes,
    takes and fakes, hides, tides,
faraway views, violences.

EVERYDAY TO HIDE

waking up to hide
word or talking to hide
how are you? to hide
seeing or hearing to hide
see you later? to hide
yeah at the shop to hide
emailing mum to hide
how you feel? to hide
it's really messed up to hide
lactose problem to hide
those fuckers! to hide
what's that soup? to hide
other sickness to hide
other wonder to hide
dentist appointment to hide
maybe museum to hide
wanna come? to hide
looking up sardinia to hide
funny cat pics to hide
a better day at work to hide
bad day at work to hide
I do love you to hide
I don't love you to hide
I'm not so sure to hide
then it's not love to hide
money probs to hide
living problem to hide
maybe go hunting to hide
or my friends to hide
accomplishments to hide
are you sadder? to hide
or recovering? to hide
and christmas to hide
remembrance day to hide
talking sexual to hide
our agreements to hide
to have a baby to hide
worried about baby to hide
and the costs to hide
the opinions to hide
ok I bought one to hide
after liking it to hide
all the proof to show
sorry I meant to hide
are we the same? to hide
be there soon to hide
bus or car ride to hide
I just think to hide

Late

There's a small image
on the back of the book
that I can't make out.

I try to expand it with my fingers.

What's happening?

There's a small image
in my head I extend into my life
of me in a computer
evolving out of me.

There's a small image
inside the computer
of me telling it what to do
and who is who.

What's happening?, says one desiring the other.

There's an image of a poem
wondering from your life
to my fingers into space screening
and spreading between
us or us or us.

The image leaves,
we turn off until something
turns it back on,
unflesh yourself darling

before too late.

Wind

Wind, why do you always try,
   why the endless sighing,
don't you realize we can't see you
   without any clothing?

Under a tree shaking with myself
   I hear the answers I need:
everything's okay, everything passes or grows.

Cold and fast you whistle-scream,
   making us bow our head
and shut the eye: dream your mum
   is helping you sleep.

Breathing in circles or straighter lines
   isn't your secret longing
to change awhile, into a shape we can see?

Soft and warm you whisper-hum,
   brushing us with our sun
so nothing can hide: wonder
   what I did in my life.

Walking into you, you split to let me
   and then seal up again,
swallowing me in your mind.

Hot and heavy you simmer-moan,
   stuffing us into ourselves
so we can't breathe: shed my skin
   to sink with my sea.

Cry over yourself, in and out
   and through yourself,
say a prayer for your dying
   which won't stay.

Or undress yourself now
   and rest inside me,
it's not too late.

BADANJILING

the eye follows the line
the wind makes the line
the sand keeps the line

the sand goes and sand stays
the sand curves and sand waits
the sand holds and sand shapes

desert family isolated and connected in ways we aren't
we're isolated and connected in ways they aren't

the light shapes the shape
the shapes shape the light

a festival of tiny beetles one bird ten flies
several camels three humans twice

the light goes everywhere it can
the sand goes everywhere it can
the wind goes everywhere it can

the line shades the light
the line lights the shade
the shade lines the light
the light lines the shade

OPENED

I got broken open.

By me. By her. By love. By loss.

By friends. By strangers. By time.

I know how it happened but I don't know why
except I needed it
                asked for it
                              to be myself again.

I broke open so well and so far I didn't need
to come back
                I didn't need
                              to close-up again.

Everything I didn't want to be gave up and released me.

And someone better stayed
                          exploded inside
                                            coming deep
in my bones
                I didn't need
                              to think it.

I opened so well my instincts grew through my heart
and in every cell
                      into my head
                                  and out my eyes.

They made peace with each other and whatever they saw.

And I glowed.
                I spilled out.
                              People looked at me
felt something
                and asked
                            what happened?

And I closed my eyes and called myself out
to hear again
                to see again.

I swallowed my eyes and saw everyone
was beautiful
                no one insane.

I opened my eyes
                called myself
in and out
                at the same time.

I wasn't split anymore.

I wasn't broken.

40 (SF TO LA)

Midnight at forty,
    dark city, dark country,
but sleep now, sleep,
    in a few more hours
there will be a plane
    and sunshine and another day,
where you will wade
    in warmer and thicker air
and toss off dreams
    along desert streets,
thirsty to the finish,
    your empire curving
in now, assembling
    in databanks,
your body waiting
    to go off.

SHIFTING OVER HER

Shifts of us were huddled over evening papers
because of some coil suddenly loosened, put back

in a child's dream of a very powerful person -

she was the fear and the dim sense of us, she
drew the fire of our most selfish delights, put out

with the breath of figures tripping on might -

now each in her winter, eyes of ease still pick up
an erasure, wipe away the sleep of screams

or laughter.

Battery

Don't build a memorial
if you don't want more war,

no matter the suffering of victims,
their friends and their families,

no matter the suffering of victims,
the killers and their helpers - however true

their ignorance and repentance.
We and the future need that neglect.

Its disabling anguish will serve us well.
It will fester inside the innocent.

There will be tremendous pain
from just the thought of inflicting

it again. Discussion of such
could happen in asylums

or graveyards perhaps.

Racket

that dog walks differently since the queen died
                nothing has changed since Chris Kaba died
those swimmers swim different since the queen died
                except Chris Kaba still dead and by police
that cloud behaves different since queen died
                nothing different for police as usual no arrest
your cock tastes different since the queen died
                nothing different by police more killings as usual
my cock taste different since the queen died
                and everything the same because – see queue
that car looks different since queen died
                except Chris Kaba got died and by police – again
that car talks different since the queen died
                except family, friends, us – see race, class, gender, etc
that dog talks different once queen died
                nothing changed since last time too – again
chuck stinks better once that queen is died
                all same since Chris Kaba died by police/system
this poem stinks nice since "queen" died
                except Chris Kaba gone people sad angry
flowers die so beautifully for the queen's die
                Chris Kaba gone and police go on, like death
and queen never queued in all long life
                Chris Kaba is dead, machine goes on
queen is queue dead/alive seen/unseen
                and Chris Kabas
                dying around us
                every day and way

DC Memorial

best war poem yet

half-written half-working so
excavate the other side to nick

the names of another

SEEDS

    I still can't believe
      you're gone

    not just far away
      or for awhile

    but locked out of time
      and out of space

    and yet as long as I grow
      you're growing

    and growing without
      knowing it

    like I did before
      I was born

    . . .

    I can't
      reach you

    you can't
      ever come back

    but sometimes
      I see with your eyes

    or listen
      with your ears

    or I think
      a thought of yours

    so I guess
      what you did

    does last
      and spread

from nothing

a little light went on
pulsed and begged
and then went off a bit later

a little light burned beside the others
but alone as they all were

and so it's pleasing to know
I'll be going home
going without seeing

to the old infinite world
of endless nothing

where I won't

Notes

This collection, like my first, spans many years. Many poems here did not fit that collection but I felt they were good/useful enough to be published. I've added recent work and tried to put it in an interesting sequence, instead of sectioning it, simply as a challenge and a different thing from before. One poem is in a different size because I felt it helped its reading if it fit on one page. Please feel free to change pronouns in the poems as you like.

Still – The Parthenon sculptures have yet to be returned to Greece despite being requested many times.

Options ... refers to a poem that can be found in *Writers Forum e-zine* (2)

Desert Island Bliss – Stemming from a BBC radio program in, I think, the early 1990s, which was about the long-running UK radio program called *Desert Island Discs*.

Greetings – Based on Israel bombing Lebanon in 2006 and photographs of Israeli missiles before launch, seen on the web, citation not kept.

Gliding with the Hitler Youth – Based on a photo at an exhibit at the Southbank Centre, London, in the 1990s. Photographer unknown.

£10 / 10 Years Old – Based on a newspaper article, late 1980s, citation lost.

Crick Institute – A research institute in London. *The possibilities are endless* was part of the information written on the hoarding during part of the time it was being constructed before opening in 2016.

Computered and **Comfuse** are detourns of previously published work with different titles.

Everyday to Hide – This is in light of the Edward Snowden revelations (2013) and the pro-surveillance propaganda, 'If you have nothing to hide you have nothing to fear.'

Racket – Chris Kaba was murdered by police in London on 5/09/22

Opened – This poem forms the second part of a loose diptych with *Broken*, published in *Inside to Outside*.

Shifting Over Her – The day Thatcher resigned, 22/11/1990.

DC Memorial – Based on the Vietnam memorial in Washington DC but could be any such memorial.

Seeds – To my father.

www.ingramcontent.com/pod-product-compliance
Lightning Source LLC
Chambersburg PA
CBHW011758040426
42446CB00019B/3461